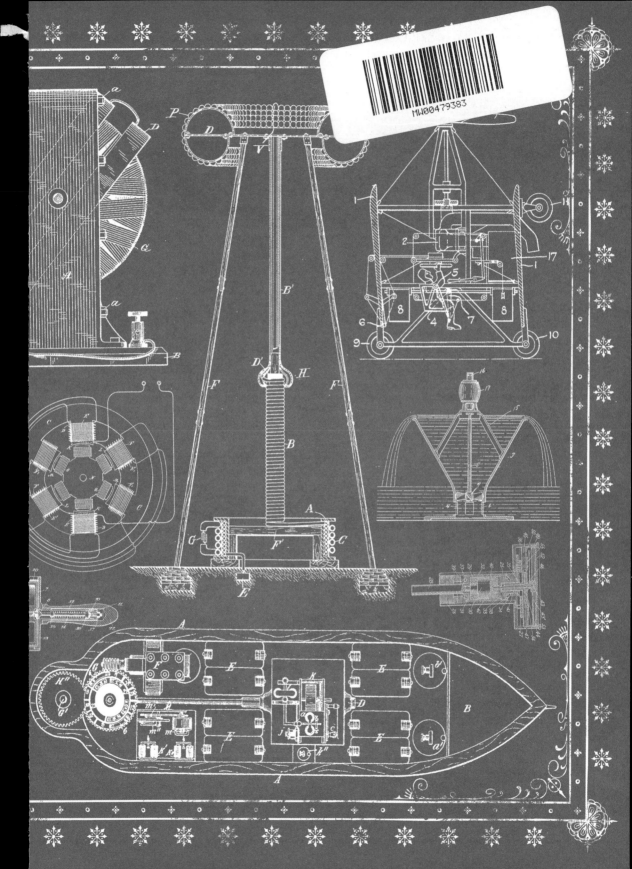

"LET THE FUTURE TELL THE
TRUTH AND EVALUATE EACH
ONE ACCORDING TO HIS WORK
AND ACCOMPLISHMENTS.
THE PRESENT IS THEIRS; THE
FUTURE, FOR WHICH I HAVE
REALLY WORKED, IS MINE."

(No Model.)

No. 335,787.

Patented Feb. 9, 1886.

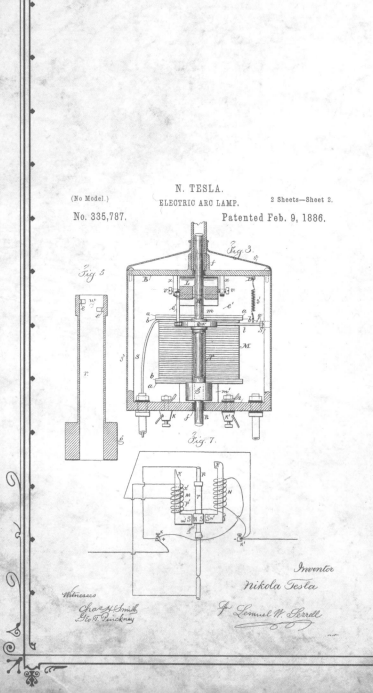

Fig. 3.

Fig. 5

Fig. 7.

Inventor

Nikola Tesla

p. Lemuel W. Serrell

Witnesses

Chas. H. Smith
Geo. T. Pinckney

"Technical invention is akin to architecture and the experts must in time come to the same conclusions I have reached long ago."

N. TESLA.

ELECTRO MAGNETIC MOTOR.

No. 381,968.   Patented May 1, 1888.

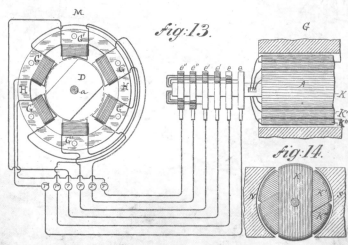

fig:13.

fig:14.

"SCIENCE IS BUT A PERVERSION
OF ITSELF UNLESS IT HAS
AS ITS ULTIMATE GOAL THE
BETTERMENT OF HUMANITY."

N. TESLA.

SYSTEM OF ELECTRICAL DISTRIBUTION.

No. 381,970.   Patented May 1, 1888.

Fig: 1.

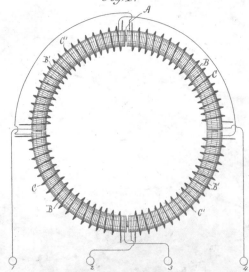

"THE DESIRE THAT GUIDES ME
IN ALL I DO IS THE DESIRE TO
HARNESS THE FORCES OF NATURE
TO THE SERVICE OF MANKIND."

N. TESLA.

ELECTRO MAGNETIC MOTOR.

No. 382,279.

Patented May 1, 1888.

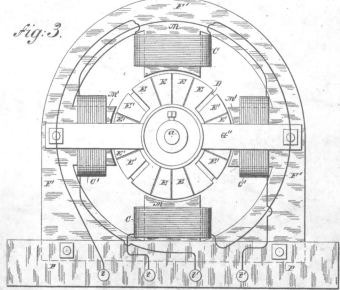

Fig. 3.

INVENTOR.

Nikola Tesla.

"THE PRACTICAL SUCCESS
OF AN IDEA, IRRESPECTIVE
OF ITS INHERENT MERIT, IS
DEPENDENT ON THE ATTITUDE
OF THE CONTEMPORARIES."

N. TESLA.

(No Model.)   DYNAMO ELECTRIC MACHINE.   2 Sheets—Sheet 2.

No. 390,414.   Patented Oct. 2, 1888.

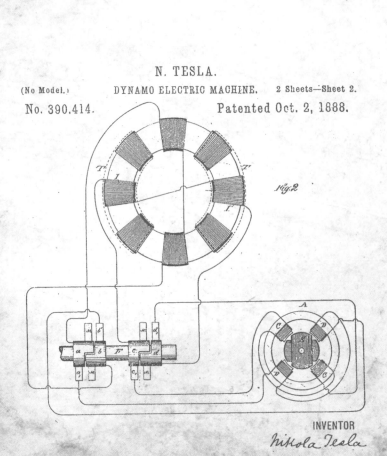

Fig.2

INVENTOR

Nikola Tesla

"WHEN WIRELESS IS PERFECTLY
APPLIED THE WHOLE EARTH
WILL BE CONVERTED INTO
A HUGE BRAIN ..."

(No Model.)

N. TESLA.

DYNAMO ELECTRIC MACHINE OR MOTOR.

No. 390,415. Patented Oct. 2, 1888.

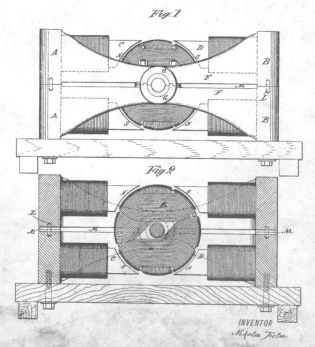

Fig.1

Fig.2

INVENTOR

Nikola Tesla

"... DO ME, AT LEAST, THE JUSTICE
OF CALLING ME AN INVENTOR
OF SOME BEAUTIFUL PIECES
OF ELECTRICAL APPARATUS."

REGULATOR FOR ALTERNATE CURRENT MOTORS.

No. 390,820.   Patented Oct. 9, 1888.

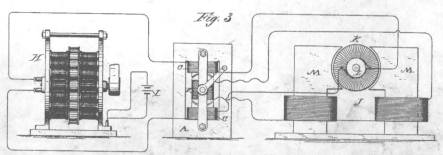

Fig. 3

INVENTOR.

Nikola Tesla

"My project was retarded by laws of nature. The world was not prepared for it. It was too far ahead of time."

N. TESLA.

THERMO MAGNETIC MOTOR.

No. 396,121. Patented Jan. 15, 1889.

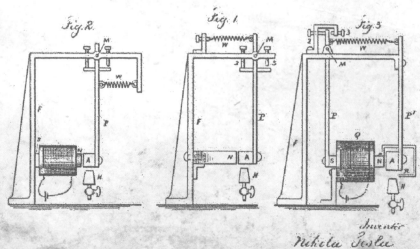

Fig. 2.   Fig. 1.   Fig. 3.

Inventor
Nikola Tesla

"We all make mistakes,
and it is better to make
them before we begin."

(No Model.)

N. TESLA.
ELECTRO MAGNETIC MOTOR.

No. 405,858.

Patented June 25, 1889.

Fig. 1

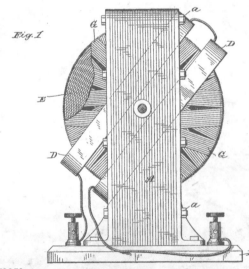

WITNESSES:

Raphael Netter

Robt. F. Gaylord

INVENTOR

Nikola Tesla

BY

Duncan, Curtis & Page

ATTORNEYS.

"OUR SENSES ENABLE
US TO PERCEIVE ONLY A
MINUTE PORTION OF THE
OUTSIDE WORLD."

N. TESLA.

METHOD OF OPERATING ELECTRO MAGNETIC MOTORS.

No. 416,192.   Patented Dec. 3, 1889.

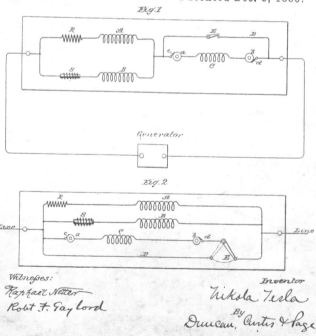

Fig.1

Generator

Fig. 2

Witnesses:

Raphael Netter

Robt. F. Gaylord

Inventor

Nikola Tesla

By

Duncan, Curtis & Page

Attorneys.

"Our virtues and our failings are inseparable, like force and matter. When they separate, man is no more."

(No Model.)

N. TESLA.
ELECTRIC MOTOR.

No. 416,194.

Patented Dec. 3, 1889.

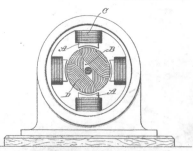

Witnesses:

Raphael Netter

Robt. F. Gaylord

Inventor

Nikola Tesla

By

Duncan, Curtis & Page

Attorneys.

"YOU MAY LIVE TO SEE
MAN-MADE HORRORS BEYOND
YOUR COMPREHENSION."

N. TESLA.
ELECTRO MAGNETIC MOTOR.

No. 418,248.　　　　　　　Patented Dec. 31, 1889.

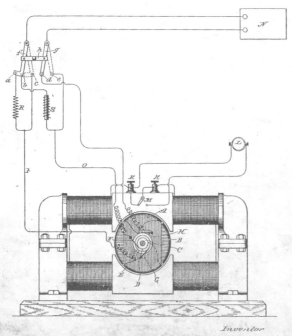

Inventor

Nikola Tesla

"THOUGH FREE TO THINK
AND ACT, WE ARE HELD
TOGETHER, LIKE THE STARS
IN THE FIRMAMENT, WITH
TIES INSEPARABLE."

(No Model.)

N. TESLA.
PYROMAGNETO ELECTRIC GENERATOR.

No. 428,057. Patented May 13, 1890.

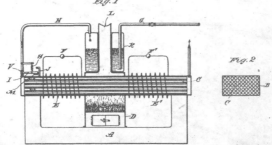

Fig. 1

Fig. 2

Witnesses
Raphael Netter
William H. Shipley

Inventor
Nikola Tesla
By
Duncan, Curtis & Page
Attorneys

"IF YOU ONLY KNEW THE
MAGNIFICENCE OF THE 3, 6
AND 9, THEN YOU WOULD HAVE
THE KEY TO THE UNIVERSE."

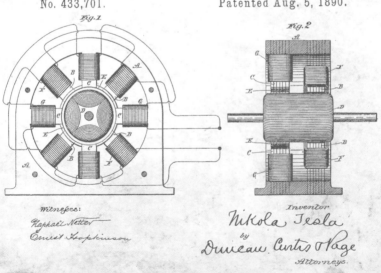

(No Model.)

N. TESLA.
ALTERNATING CURRENT MOTOR.

No. 433,701.

Patented Aug. 5, 1890.

Fig.1

Fig.2

Witnesses:
Raphael Netter
Ernest Hopkinson

Inventor
Nikola Tesla
by
Duncan, Curtis & Page
Attorneys.

"OF ALL THE FRICTIONAL
RESISTANCES, THE ONE
THAT MOST RETARDS HUMAN
MOVEMENT IS IGNORANCE ..."

N. TESLA.
ALTERNATING ELECTRIC CURRENT GENERATOR.

No. 447,921.   Patented Mar. 10, 1891.

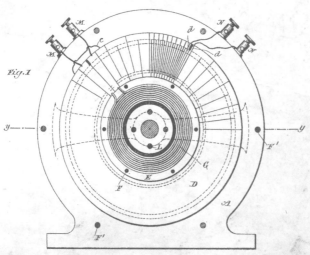

Fig.1

Witnesses:
Ernest Hopkinson
Frank B. Murphy.

Inventor
Nikola Tesla
by
Duncan & Page
Attorneys.

"THE SCIENTIFIC MAN DOES NOT AIM AT AN IMMEDIATE RESULT ... HE LIVES AND LABORS AND HOPES."

(No Model.)

N. TESLA.
ELECTRIC INCANDESCENT LAMP.

No. 455,069.   Patented June 30, 1891.

Fig. 2

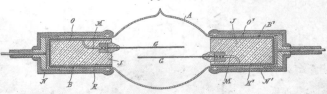

Inventor
Nikola Tesla
by
Duncan & Page
Attorneys.

"I DO NOT THINK THERE IS
ANY THRILL THAT CAN GO
THROUGH THE HUMAN HEART
LIKE THAT FELT BY THE
INVENTOR AS HE SEES SOME
CREATION OF THE BRAIN
UNFOLDING TO SUCCESS ..."

N. TESLA.
SYSTEM OF ELECTRICAL TRANSMISSION OF POWER.

No. 487,796.   Patented Dec. 13, 1892.

Fig. 3   *Fig. 4*

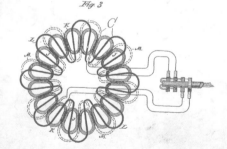
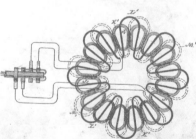

WITNESSES:

Raphael Netter

Allan W. Paige

INVENTOR

Nikola Tesla

BY

Duncan, Curtis & Page

ATTORNEYS.

"THE SCIENTISTS OF TODAY THINK
DEEPLY INSTEAD OF CLEARLY.
ONE MUST BE SANE TO THINK
CLEARLY, BUT ONE CAN THINK
DEEPLY AND BE QUITE INSANE."

(No Model.)

N. TESLA.
ELECTRICAL TRANSMISSION OF POWER.

No. 511,559.   Patented Dec. 26, 1893.

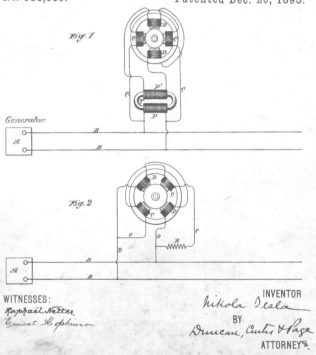

Fig. 1

Generator.

Fig. 2

WITNESSES:
Raphaël Netter
Ernest Hopkinson

INVENTOR
Nikola Tesla
BY
Duncan, Curtis & Page
ATTORNEYS.

"It has cost me years of thought to arrive at certain results, by many believed to be unattainable ..."

(No Model.)

N. TESLA.

INCANDESCENT ELECTRIC LIGHT.

No. 514,170.

Patented Feb. 6, 1894.

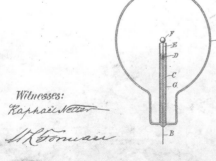

Witnesses:

Raphaël Netter

M. K. Forman

Inventor

Nikola Tesla

by

Duncan & Page

Attorneys

"I DON'T CARE THAT THEY STOLE
MY IDEA ... I CARE THAT THEY
DON'T HAVE ANY OF THEIR OWN."

(No Model.)

N. TESLA.
ELECTRIC RAILWAY SYSTEM.

No. 514,972.

Patented Feb. 20, 1894.

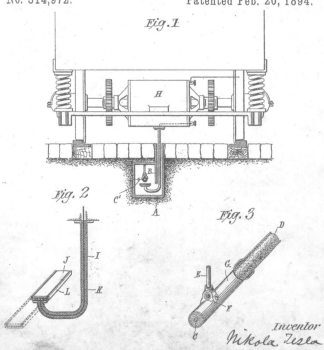

Fig. 1

Fig. 2

Fig. 3

Inventor

Nikola Tesla

"IF YOU WANT TO FIND THE
SECRETS OF THE UNIVERSE,
THINK IN TERMS OF ENERGY,
FREQUENCY AND VIBRATION."

N. TESLA.
ALTERNATING MOTOR.

No. 555,190. Patented Feb. 25, 1896.

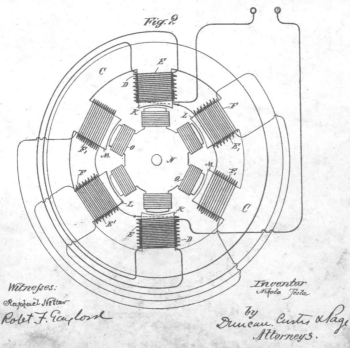

Fig. 2

Witnesses:
Raphaël Netter
Robert F. Gaylord

Inventor
Nikola Tesla
by
Duncan, Curtis & Page
Attorneys.

"IF YOUR HATE COULD BE TURNED
INTO ELECTRICITY, IT WOULD
LIGHT UP THE WHOLE WORLD."

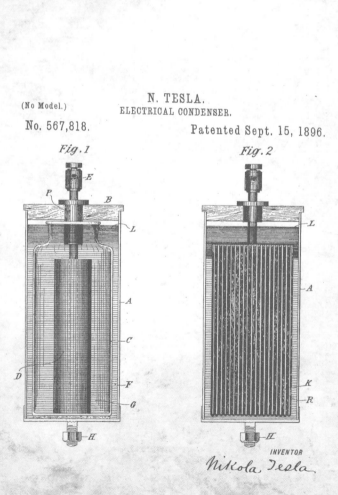

Fig. 1   Fig. 2

INVENTOR

Nikola Tesla

"OF ALL THINGS,
I LIKED BOOKS BEST."

(No Model.) N. TESLA. 2 Sheets—Sheet 2.

APPARATUS FOR PRODUCING ELECTRIC CURRENTS OF HIGH FREQUENCY AND POTENTIAL.

No. 568,176. Patented Sept. 22, 1896.

Fig. 2

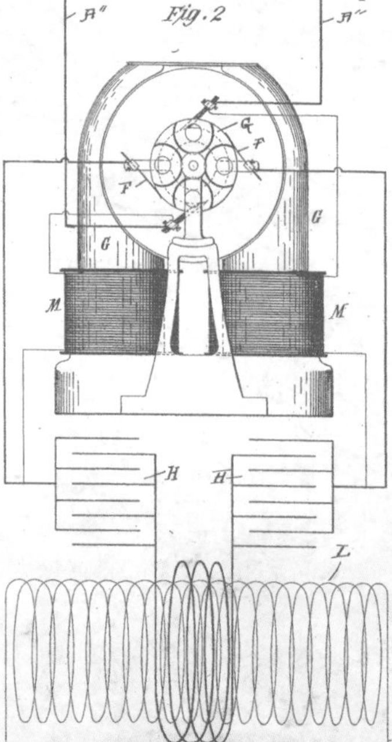

Nikola Tesla INVENTOR

"LIFE IS AND WILL EVER REMAIN
AN EQUATION INCAPABLE OF
SOLUTION, BUT IT CONTAINS
CERTAIN KNOWN FACTORS."

N. TESLA.
APPARATUS FOR PRODUCING OZONE.

No. 568,177.　　　　　　　　　Patented Sept. 22, 1896.

Fig.1

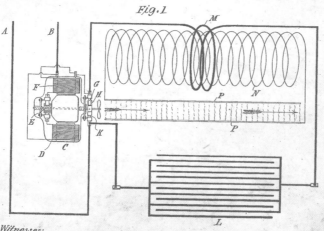

"INVENTION IS THE MOST
IMPORTANT PRODUCT OF
MAN'S CREATIVE BRAIN."

N. TESLA.
ELECTRICAL TRANSFORMER.

No. 593,138.   Patented Nov. 2, 1897.

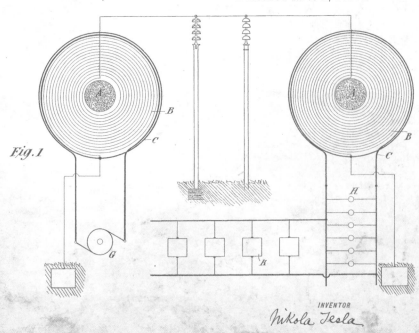

Fig.1

INVENTOR

Nikola Tesla

"THE WONDERS OF
YESTERDAY ARE TODAY
COMMON OCCURRENCES"

No. 613,809.

N. TESLA.

Patented Nov. 8, 1898.

METHOD OF AND APPARATUS FOR CONTROLLING MECHANISM OF MOVING VESSELS
OR VEHICLES.

(No Model.)

5 Sheets—Sheet I.

Fig.1

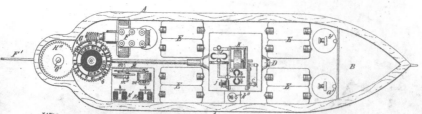

Witnesses:
Raphaël Netter
George Scheff.

Inventor
Nikola Tesla

"BE ALONE, THAT IS THE SECRET
OF INVENTION; BE ALONE, THAT
IS WHEN IDEAS ARE BORN."

No. 613,809. Patented Nov. 8, 1898.

N. TESLA.

METHOD OF AND APPARATUS FOR CONTROLLING MECHANISM OF MOVING VESSELS OR VEHICLES.

(No Model.)

Fig. 4

Fig. 8

Fig. 7

Witnesses:
Raphaël Netter
George Scherff.

Inventor:
Nikola Tesla

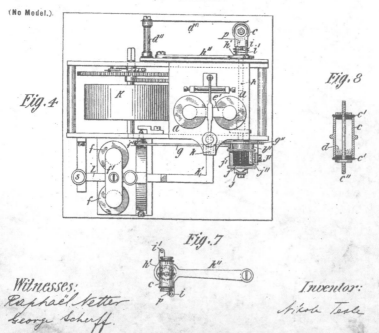

"WHAT ONE MAN CALLS
GOD, ANOTHER CALLS THE
LAWS OF PHYSICS."

No. 645,576.　　　　　　　　　　　　　　Patented Mar. 20, 1900.
N. TESLA.
SYSTEM OF TRANSMISSION OF ELECTRICAL ENERGY.
(Application filed Sept. 2, 1897.)

(No Model.)

INVENTOR

Nikola Tesla

"ANTI-SOCIAL BEHAVIOR IS
A TRAIT OF INTELLIGENCE IN A
WORLD FULL OF CONFORMISTS."

No. 655,838.

N. TESLA.

Patented Aug. 14, 1900.

METHOD OF INSULATING ELECTRIC CONDUCTORS.

(Application filed June 15, 1900.)

(No Model.)

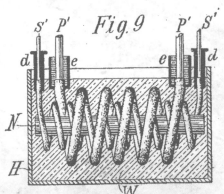

Fig.9

Witnesses:

Raphaël Netter

C. D. Morrill,

Nikola Tesla, Inventor

Kerr, Page & Cooper,

by

Att'ys

"EVERY LIVING BEING IS AN
ENGINE GEARED TO THE
WHEELWORK OF THE UNIVERSE."

No. 685,012.

Patented Oct. 22, 1901.

N. TESLA.

MEANS FOR INCREASING THE INTENSITY OF ELECTRICAL OSCILLATIONS.

(Application filed Mar. 21, 1900. Renewed July 3, 1901.)

(No Model.)

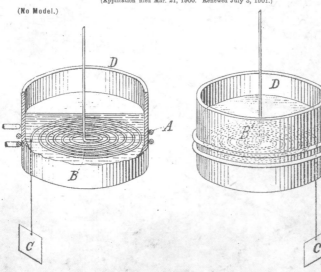

"... THE UNIVERSE IS SIMPLY
A GREAT MACHINE WHICH
NEVER CAME INTO BEING
AND NEVER WILL END."

No. 685,953.

Patented Nov. 5, 1901.

N. TESLA.

METHOD OF INTENSIFYING AND UTILIZING EFFECTS TRANSMITTED THROUGH NATURAL MEDIA.

(No Model.)

(Application filed June 24, 1899. Renewed May 29, 1901.)

Fig. I.

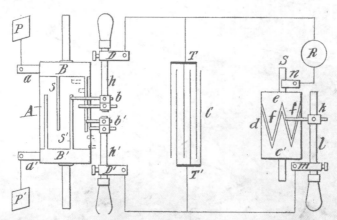

Witnesses:

G. B. Lewis.

Hellary C. Messimer.

Nikola Tesla, Inventor

by Kerr, Page & Cooper
Att'ys

"... INSTINCT IS SOMETHING
WHICH TRANSCENDS
KNOWLEDGE."

No. 685,956.

Patented Nov. 5, 1901.

N. TESLA.
APPARATUS FOR UTILIZING EFFECTS TRANSMITTED THROUGH NATURAL MEDIA.

(Application filed Nov. 2, 1899. Renewed May 29, 1901.)

(No Model.)

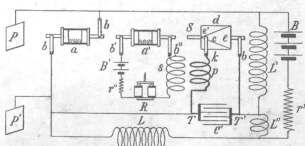

Witnesses:

Raphaël Netter

M. Lawson Dyer.

Inventor

Nikola Tesla

by Kerr, Page & Cooper, Attorneys.

"THE HUMAN MIND THINKS BUT
TO COMPLICATE. AS SOON
AS ONE PROBLEM IS SOLVED,
THAT SOLUTION INTRODUCES
NEW COMPLICATIONS ..."

No. 685,958.   N. TESLA.   Patented Nov. 5, 1901.

METHOD OF UTILIZING RADIANT ENERGY.

(No Model.)   (Application filed Mar. 21, 1901.)

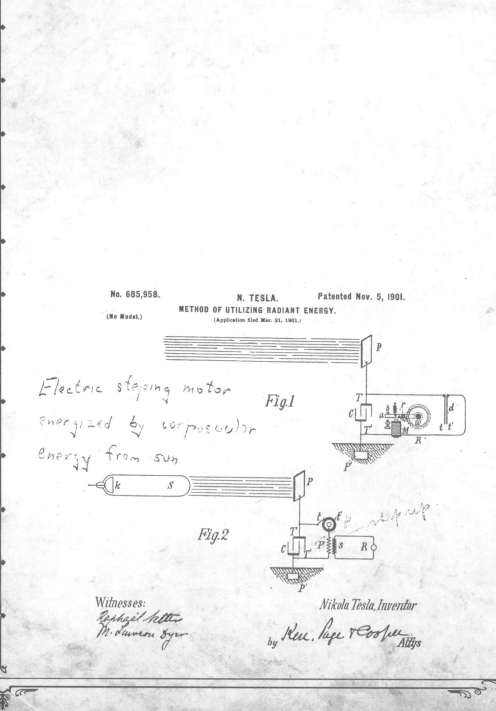

Electric steping motor energized by corpuscular energy from sun

Fig.1

Fig.2

Nikola Tesla, Inventor

Witnesses:

Raphaël Netter

M. Lawson Dyer

by Kerr. Page & Cooper

Attys

"A NEW IDEA MUST
NOT BE JUDGED BY ITS
IMMEDIATE RESULTS."

N. TESLA.

SYSTEM OF SIGNALING.

NO MODEL.

No. 725,605.

APPLICATION FILED JULY 16, 1900.

PATENTED APR. 14, 1903.

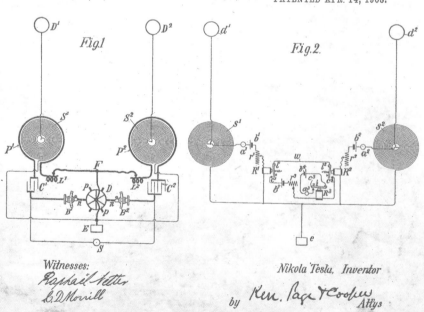

Fig.1

Fig.2

Witnesses:

Raphael Netter

C. D. Morrill

Nikola Tesla, Inventor

by Ken. Page & Cooper

Attys

"WE BUILD BUT TO TEAR DOWN ... OUR ONWARD MARCH IS MARKED BY DEVASTATION ... A CHEERLESS VIEW, BUT TRUE."

No. 787,412.

PATENTED APR. 18, 1905.

N. TESLA.

ART OF TRANSMITTING ELECTRICAL ENERGY THROUGH THE NATURAL
MEDIUMS.

APPLICATION FILED MAY 16, 1900. RENEWED JUNE 17, 1902.

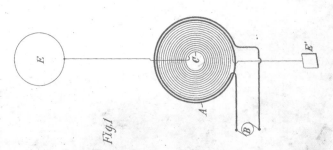

Fig.1

Witnesses:

Raphaël Netter

M. Lawson Dyer.

Nikola Tesla   Inventor

by Ken, Page & Cooker Attys

"IT WILL SOON BE POSSIBLE TO
TRANSMIT WIRELESS MESSAGES
AROUND THE WORLD SO
SIMPLY THAT ANY INDIVIDUAL
CAN CARRY AND OPERATE
HIS OWN APPARATUS."

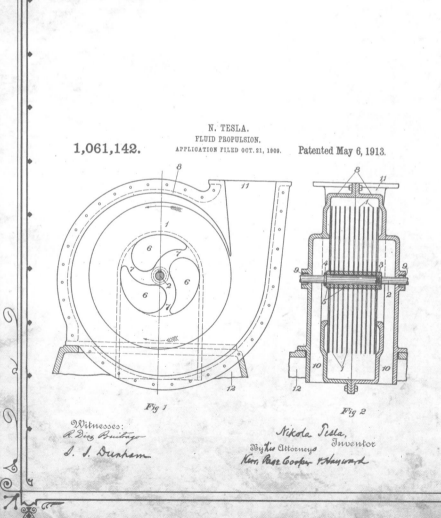

N. TESLA.

FLUID PROPULSION.

APPLICATION FILED OCT. 21, 1909.

1,061,142.

Patented May 6, 1913.

Fig 1

Fig 2

Witnesses:
R. Diez Buitrago
S. S. Dunham

Nikola Tesla, Inventor

By his Attorneys
Kerr, Page Cooper & Hayward

"... ALL EARTH MEN ARE ALIKE.
THERE IS IN FACT BUT ONE
RACE, OF MANY COLORS."

N. TESLA.

TURBINE.

APPLICATION FILED JAN. 17, 1911.

1,061,206.

Patented May 6, 1913.

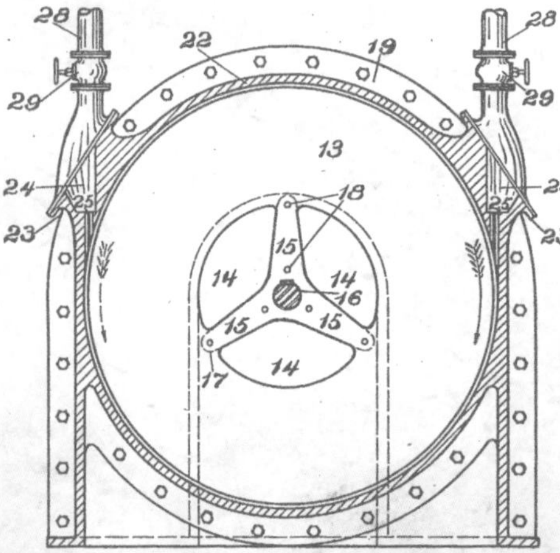

Fig. 1.

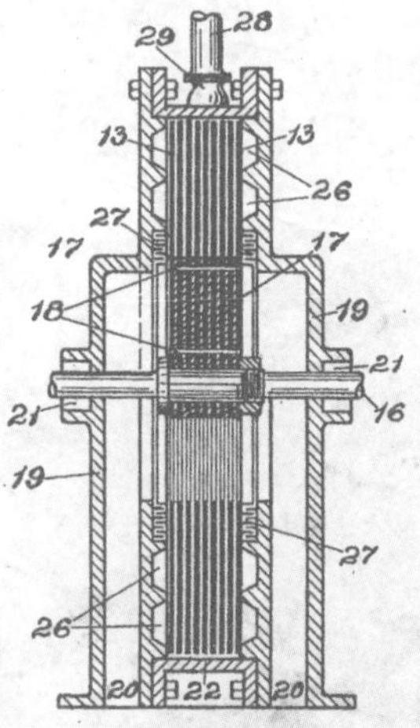

Fig. 2.

Witnesses:

R. Diaz Buitrago

Wm Cohleber

Nikola Tesla, Inventor

By his Attorneys

Kerr Page Cooper & Hayward

"IT IS PARADOXICAL, YET TRUE, TO
SAY, THAT THE MORE WE KNOW,
THE MORE IGNORANT WE BECOME
IN THE ABSOLUTE SENSE ..."

N. TESLA.

FOUNTAIN.

1,113,716. APPLICATION FILED OCT. 28, 1913. Patented Oct. 13, 1914.

2 SHEETS—SHEET 2.

Fig. 4.

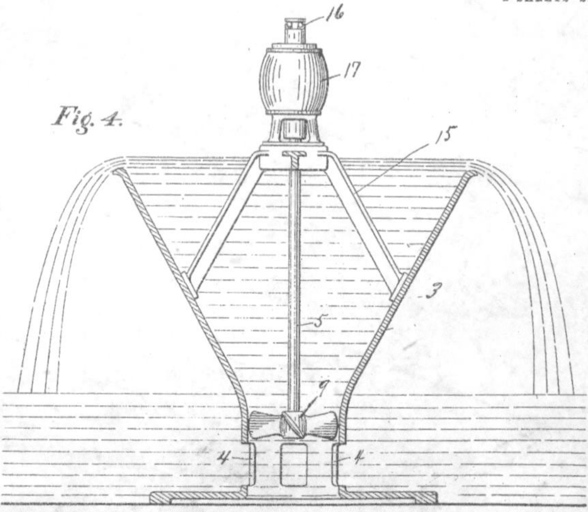

WITNESSES:

R. Diaz Buitrago

Wm Bohleber

INVENTOR.

Nikola Tesla

BY

Kerr Page Cooper & Hayward

ATTORNEYS

"EXPERIENCE IS MADE BEFORE
THE LAW IS FORMULATED,
BOTH ARE RELATED LIKE
CAUSE AND EFFECT."

N. TESLA.

APPARATUS FOR TRANSMITTING ELECTRICAL ENERGY.

APPLICATION FILED JAN. 18, 1902. RENEWED MAY 4, 1907.

1,119,732.

Patented Dec. 1, 1914.

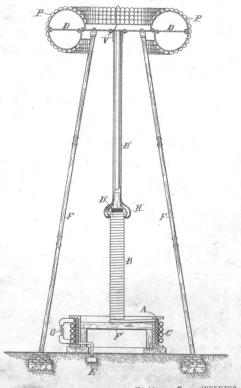

Nikola Tesla,

INVENTOR,

"MISUNDERSTANDINGS ARE
ALWAYS CAUSED BY THE
INABILITY OF APPRECIATING ONE
ANOTHER'S POINT OF VIEW."

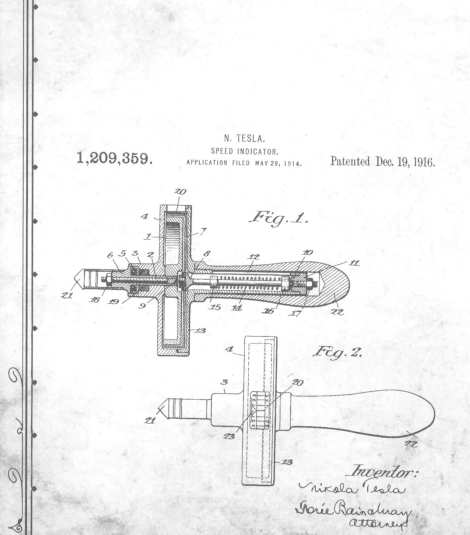

Fig. 1.

Fig. 2.

Inventor:

Nikola Tesla

Borie Rainahvay
attorney

"MUTUAL UNDERSTANDING
WOULD BE IMMENSELY
FACILITATED BY THE USE OF
ONE UNIVERSAL TONGUE.
BUT WHICH SHALL IT BE, IS
THE GREAT QUESTION."

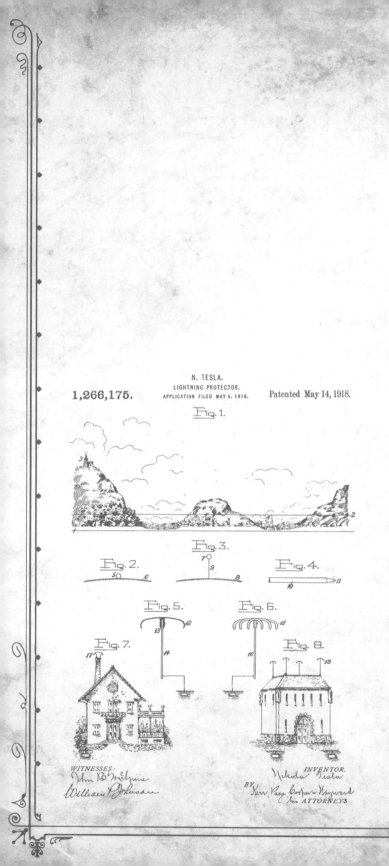

1,266,175.

N. TESLA.
LIGHTNING PROTECTOR.
APPLICATION FILED MAY 6, 1916.

Patented May 14, 1918.

Fig. 1.

Fig. 3.

Fig. 2.

Fig. 4.

Fig. 5.

Fig. 6.

Fig. 7.

Fig. 8.

WITNESSES:

John B. McIlpine

William P. Johnson

INVENTOR.

Nikola Tesla

BY

Kerr, Page, Cooper & Hayward

his ATTORNEYS

"The individual is ephemeral, races and nations come and pass away, but man remains."

N. TESLA.

SPEED INDICATOR.

APPLICATION FILED DEC. 18, 1916.

1,274,816.

Patented Aug. 6, 1918.

Fig. 2.

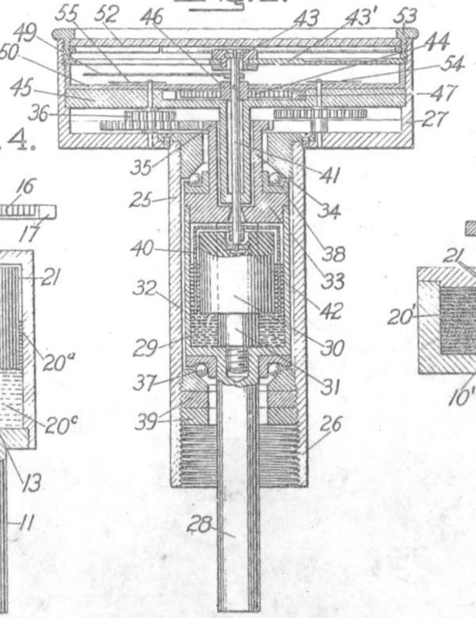

Fig. 4.

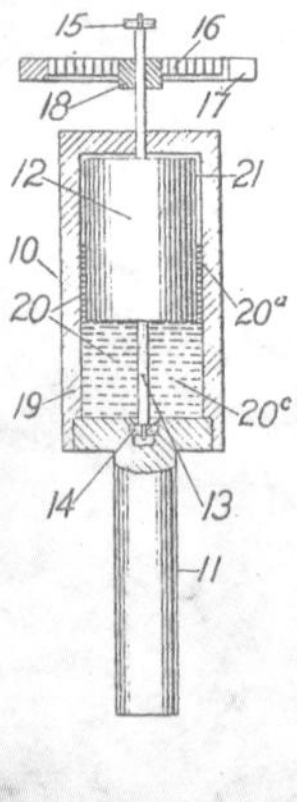

Fig. 5.

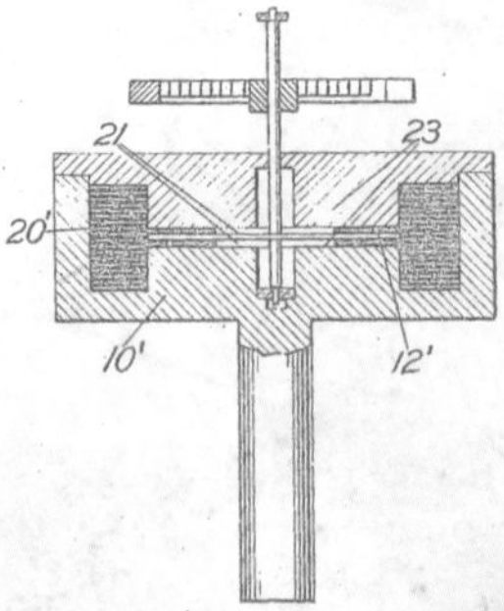

Inventor

Nikola Tesla

By his Attorneys

Forée Bain & May

"TO CONQUER BY SHEER
FORCE IS BECOMING HARDER
AND HARDER EVERY DAY."

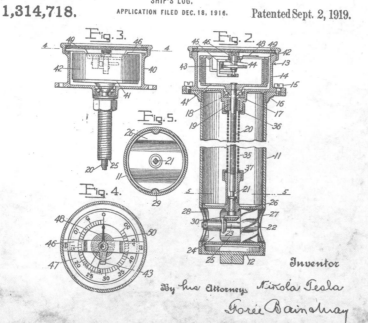

Inventor

By his Attorney   Nikola Tesla

Forée Bainbray

"IDEAS CAME IN AN UNINTERRUPTED STREAM AND THE ONLY DIFFICULTY I HAD WAS TO HOLD THEM FAST ..."

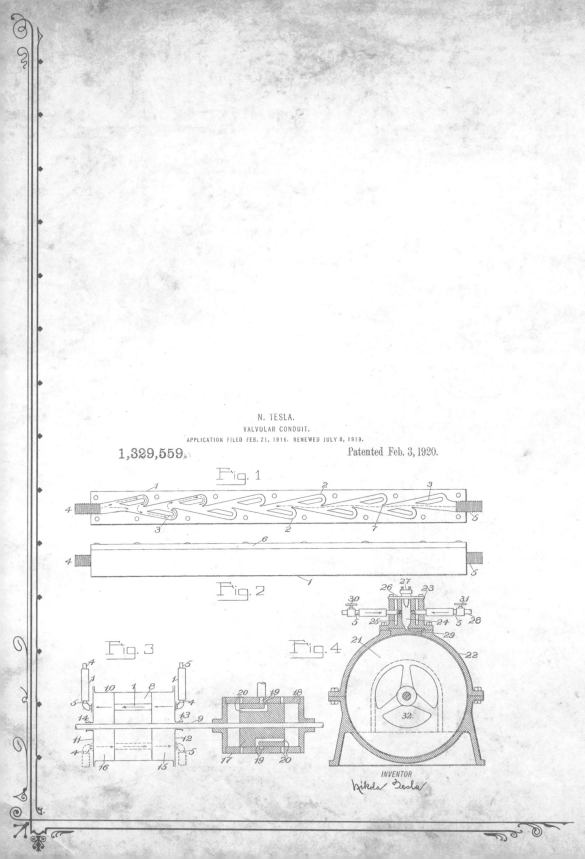

N. TESLA.
VALVULAR CONDUIT.
APPLICATION FILED FEB. 21, 1916. RENEWED JULY 8, 1919.

1,329,559.

Patented Feb. 3, 1920.

Fig. 1

Fig. 2

Fig. 3

Fig. 4

INVENTOR
Nikola Tesla

"THE FEELING IS CONSTANTLY
GROWING ON ME THAT I HAD BEEN
THE FIRST TO HEAR THE GREETING
OF ONE PLANET TO ANOTHER."

N. TESLA.

FLOW METER.

APPLICATION FILED DEC. 18, 1916.

1,365,547.

Patented Jan. 11, 1921.

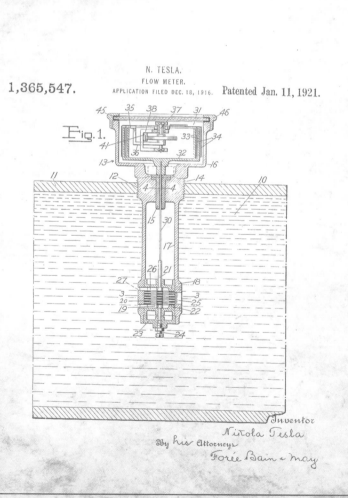

Fig. 1.

Inventor

Nikola Tesla

By his Attorneys

Foree Bain & May

"THE MIND IS SHARPER AND KEENER IN SECLUSION AND UNINTERRUPTED SOLITUDE."

1,402,025.

Patented Jan. 3, 1922.

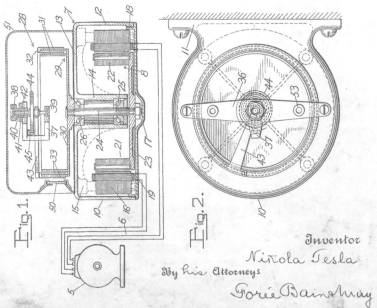

Fig. 1.

Fig. 2.

Inventor

Nikola Tesla

By his Attorneys

Foree Bainbridge

"I AM NOT AN INVENTOR.
I AM A DISCOVERER OF NEW
SCIENTIFIC PRINCIPLES."

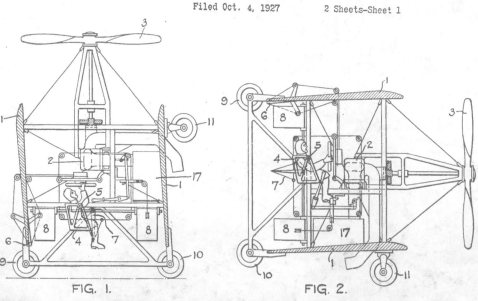

FIG. I.   FIG. 2.

INVENTOR.
NIKOLA TESLA.

"... WE ARE NOTHING BUT WAVES
IN SPACE AND TIME WHICH WHEN
DISSOLVED EXIST NO MORE."

This edition published in 2015 by
Chartwell Books
an imprint of Book Sales
a division of Quarto Publishing Group USA Inc
276 Fifth Avenue Suite 206
New York, New York 10001
USA

ISBN: 978-0-7858-3225-6

Printed in China

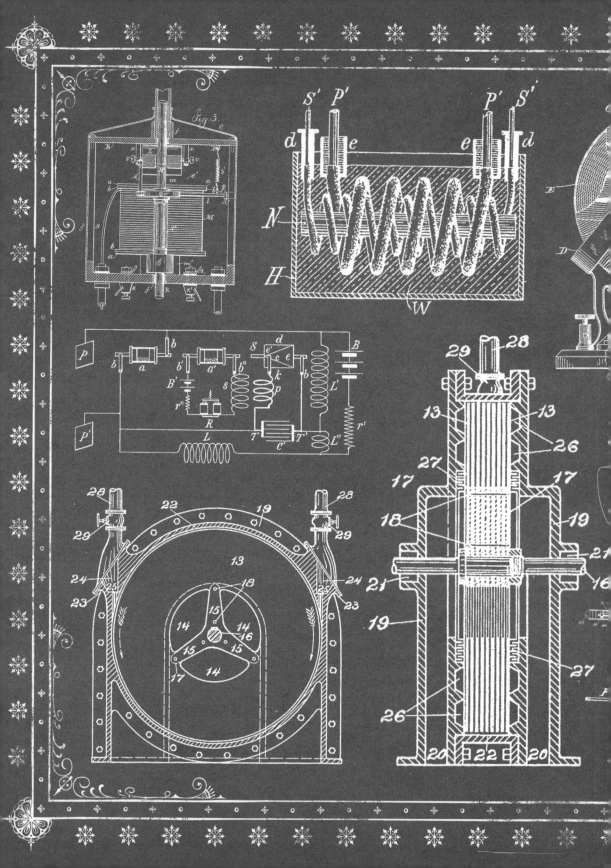